sundance publishing

LITTLE RED
READERS

Sick in Bed

PETER SLOAN &
SHERYL SLOAN

Illustrated by Virginia Barrett

I was sick and had to stay
in bed.
"Don't get up," my mother
said.
"You must rest."

My big brother came into
my room.
He had a video game.
We played the video
game.

My sister came into
my room.
She had some blocks.
We made a house.

My grandfather came into
my room.
He had a game board.
We played a game.

My grandmother came into my room.
She turned on the television.
We watched television.

My father came into
my room.
He had my crayons.
We drew some pictures.

My mother came into
my room.
She tucked me in.
"Being in bed is tiring!" I
said.